ABT

3/06

P9-EEC-588

TOM BRADY
and the
New England Patriots

SUPER BOWL XXXVIII

by Michael Sandler

Consultant: Norries Wilson
Head Football Coach
Columbia University

BEARPORT
PUBLISHING

New York, New York

Credits

Cover and Title Page, © Donald Miralle/Getty Images; 4, John Zich/NewSport/ Corbis; 5, Bob Rosato/Sports Illustrated; 6, Courtesy of Russ Bertetta, Junipero Serra High School; 7, George Rose/Getty Images; 8, James D. Smith/WireImage.com; 9, AP Photo/Gary I. Rothstein; 10, REUTERS/Jim Bourg; 11, REUTERS/Mike Segar; 12, Robert Klein/WireImage.com; 13, REUTERS/Gary Wiepert; 14, UPI Photo/Steven E. Frischling/Newscom; 15, AP Photo/Jim Rogash; 16, Jim Davis/The Boston Globe/ Redux; 17, Brian Bahr/Getty Images; 18, REUTERS/Pierre Ducharme; 19, Brian Bahr/ Getty Images; 20, Keith Nordstrom-Ai Wire/Newscom; 21, Elsa/Getty Images; 22L, Brian Bahr/Getty Images; 22R, Andy Lyons/Getty Images; 22 Background, AP Images/Mark J. Terrill.

Publisher: Kenn Goin
Senior Editor: Lisa Wiseman
Creative Director: Spencer Brinker
Design: Deborah Kaiser
Photo Researcher: Jennifer Bright

Library of Congress Cataloging-in-Publication Data

Sandler, Michael.
  Tom Brady and the New England Patriots : Super Bowl XXXVIII / by Michael Sandler.
      p. cm. — (Super bowl superstars)
  Includes bibliographical references and index.
  ISBN-13: 978-1-59716-535-8 (library binding)
  ISBN-10: 1-59716-535-2 (library binding)
  1. Brady, Tom, 1977—Juvenile literature. 2. Football players—United States— Biography—Juvenile literature. 3. Super Bowl—Juvenile literature. I. Title.

  GV939.B685S26 2008
  796.332092—dc22
  (B)
                            2007003615

For more information, write to Bearport Publishing Company, Inc., 101 Fifth Avenue, Suite 6R, New York, New York 10003. Printed in the United States of America.

10 9 8 7 6 5 4 3

★ Contents ★

Fourth Quarter Fireworks

No one could remember a Super Bowl fourth quarter like this one. Five touchdowns had already been scored. With 14 seconds left, the score between the New England Patriots and the Carolina Panthers was tied, 29-29.

The Patriots had the ball as the clock ticked down. Quarterback Tom Brady dropped back to pass. Could he set up his team for the winning score?

Tom Brady (#12) reacts happily to a first down during Super Bowl XXXVIII (38).

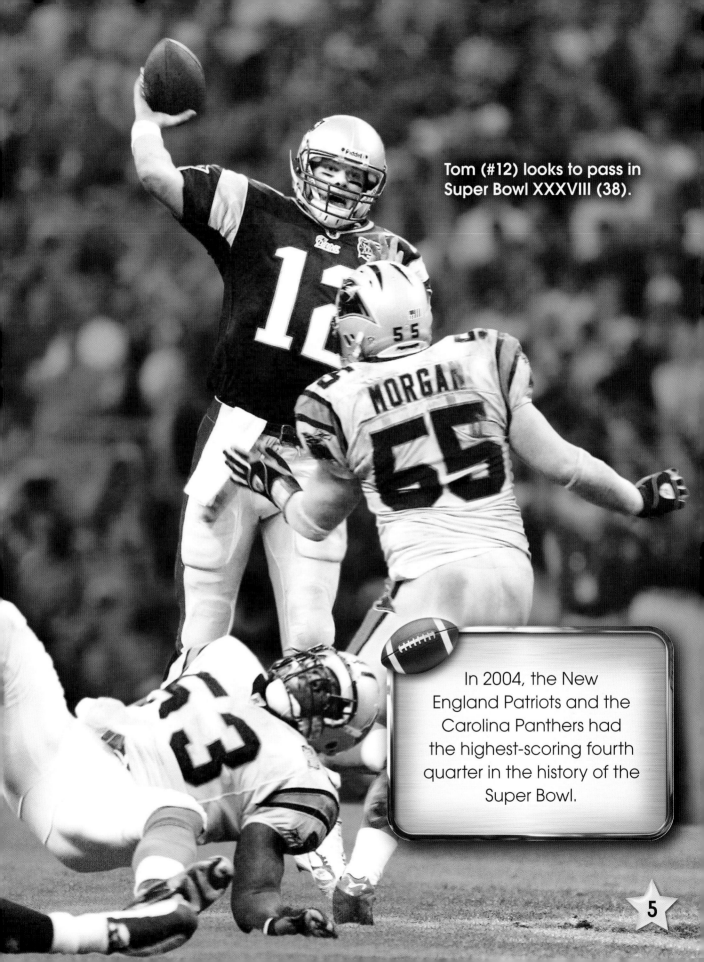

Tom (#12) looks to pass in Super Bowl XXXVIII (38).

In 2004, the New England Patriots and the Carolina Panthers had the highest-scoring fourth quarter in the history of the Super Bowl.

A Late Start

Tom Brady didn't play much football as a child. His parents wouldn't let him. They worried he might get hurt.

In ninth grade, he was finally allowed to join a team. At first, coaches made him a **backup** because he looked small and slow. Tom, though, worked hard. By senior year, he was one of San Francisco's best high school quarterbacks.

Tom grew up in San Mateo, a suburb of San Francisco, California.

Joe Montana

Growing up, Tom was a huge fan of Joe Montana. This famous quarterback led the San Francisco 49ers to four Super Bowl victories.

Waiting with the Wolverines

After high school, Tom headed to the University of Michigan. The Michigan Wolverines had many quarterbacks. For two years, Tom waited on the **sideline** for a chance to play.

When the time finally came, Tom shined. His passing was sharp. In the **pocket**, he was cool and steady like his hero Joe Montana. He set school passing records and led his team to an **Orange Bowl** win. Then, the New England Patriots picked Tom in the 2000 **draft**.

Tom (#10) holds the Michigan record for completions in a game—34.

College players are chosen by National Football League (NFL) teams in a yearly draft.

Tom throws a 27-yard (25-m) touchdown pass in the Orange Bowl.

Super Starter

With New England, Tom began as a backup once again. Then injury struck **starting** quarterback Drew Bledsoe. Tom took his place.

What happened next amazed Patriots fans. New England won game after game. They soon found themselves in Super Bowl XXXVI (36).

Despite playing in the big game, Tom seemed to feel no **pressure**. He calmly led his team to victory over the mighty St. Louis Rams.

Tom (#12) helps New England to a 44-13 victory in his very first NFL start in 2001.

Tom, only 24 years old, became the youngest quarterback ever to win a Super Bowl. Who held the record before him? Joe Montana!

Tom was named the Most Valuable Player (MVP) of Super Bowl XXXVI (36).

Tough at the Top

Now Tom was a star. He soon learned, however, that life at the top isn't easy. As team leader, Tom got blamed when things went wrong.

Fans grumbled when New England didn't make the playoffs in 2002. They grumbled even louder when the team lost the first game of the 2003 season to the Buffalo Bills. Afterward, Tom said, "We have to be better and we will be better."

Tom talks to a reporter after a game in 2002.

Tom rarely made **turnovers**. Against Buffalo, however, he threw four **interceptions**.

13

Turning It Around

Tom kept his word. The Patriots started winning and powered into the playoffs. Their first **opponents** were the Tennessee Titans. Tom threw passes to ten different **receivers**. The Patriots won, 17-14.

Next up were the Indianapolis Colts, led by star quarterback Peyton Manning. Tom outplayed Peyton as New England beat the Colts. The Patriots were heading back to the Super Bowl!

Patriots tight end Christian Fauria makes a catch during the playoff game against the Titans.

Tom signals to his teammates before a play during New England's 24-14 victory over Indianapolis.

The Patriots ended the 2003 season with 14 straight wins. A Super Bowl victory would give them 15 straight wins!

Super Bowl XXXVIII (38)

In Super Bowl XXXVIII (38), New England faced the Carolina Panthers. At first, neither team could score.

Then, late in the first half, Tom fired short touchdown passes to Deion Branch and David Givens. At halftime, the Patriots led, 14-10.

After a scoreless third quarter, Tom opened the fourth with a 71-yard (65-m) touchdown drive. The Panthers struck right back with two quick touchdowns. Carolina now had a 22-21 lead.

Tom (#12) and teammate Deion Branch (#83) celebrate their first-half touchdown.

It took 26 minutes and 55 seconds for the first points to be scored—a Super Bowl record.

DeShaun Foster (#20) leaps through the air to make a touchdown for the Panthers.

Back and Forth

The fourth quarter got even more exciting. Tom's one-yard (1-m) touchdown pass to **linebacker** Mike Vrabel gave New England the lead again.

However, Carolina scored another touchdown. The game was tied, 29-29. With a minute remaining, overtime seemed like a sure thing.

The Patriots did not want to go into overtime. They needed to get into **field goal range**. Could Tom drive them downfield before time ran out?

Mike Vrabel (#50) makes a key touchdown.

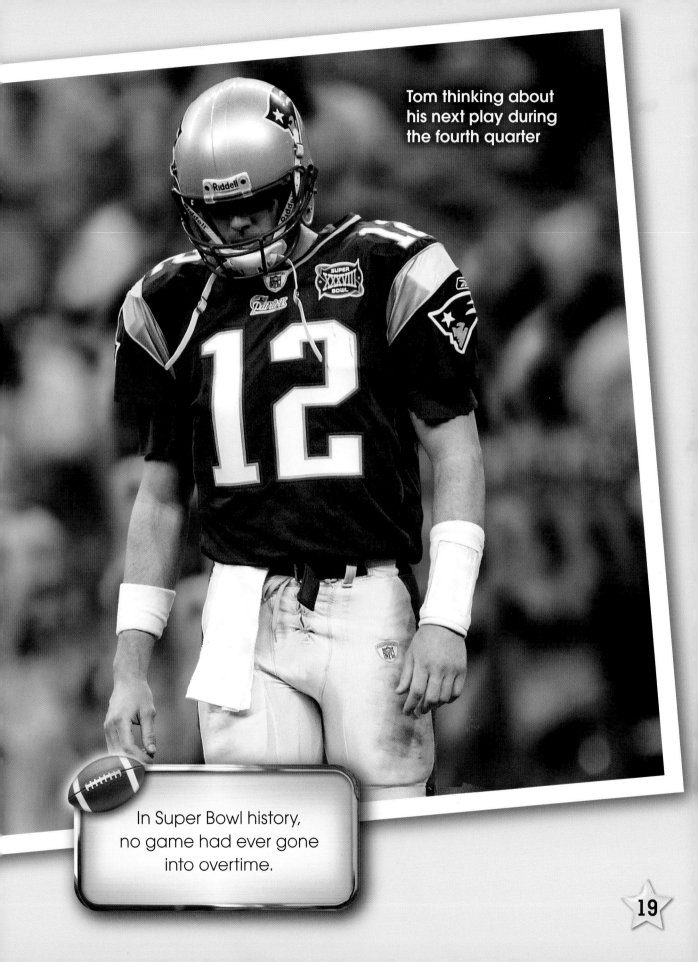

Tom thinking about his next play during the fourth quarter

In Super Bowl history, no game had ever gone into overtime.

Tom's Moment

With 14 seconds left, Tom fired the ball to Deion Branch for a 17-yard (16-m) gain. The Patriots were in field goal range!

Tom had done his job. Now it was up to the **kicker**, Adam Vinatieri. He had already blown two easy kicks. This time, however, he blasted the ball through the **uprights**.

Tom and Adam jumped into the air. The Patriots had won Super Bowl XXXVIII (38)!

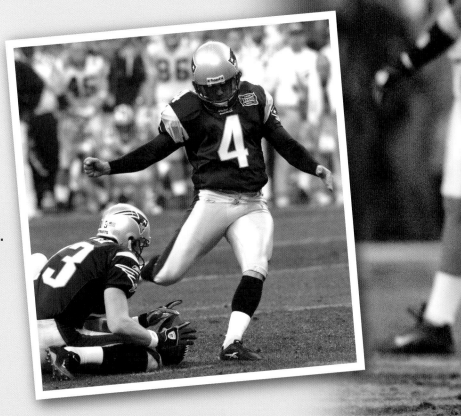

Adam Vinatieri (#4) kicked the winning field goal for the Patriots.

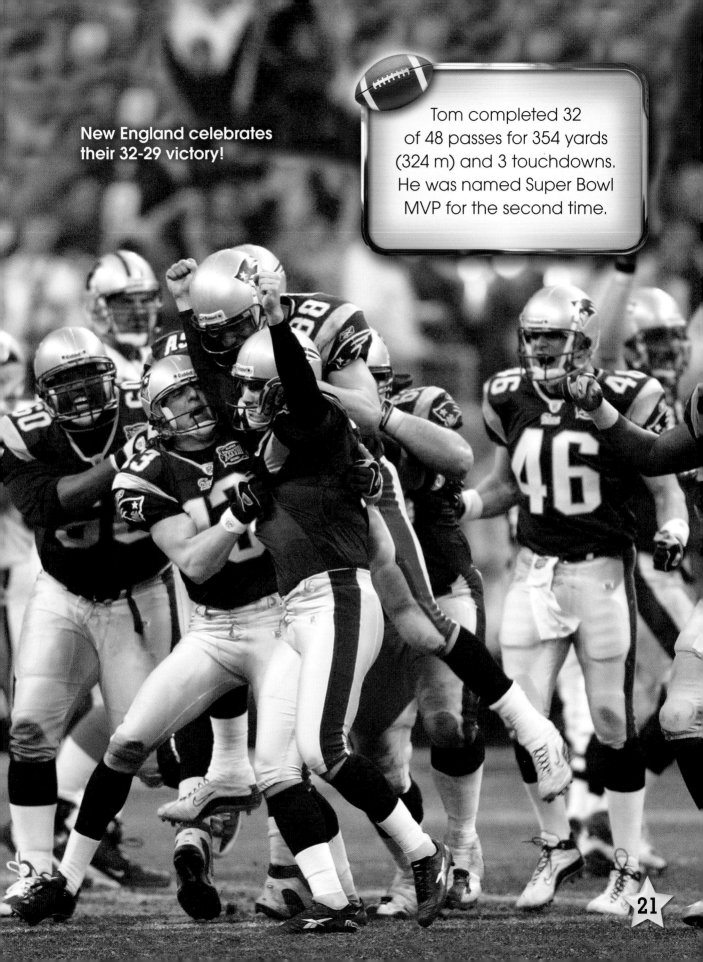

New England celebrates their 32-29 victory!

Tom completed 32 of 48 passes for 354 yards (324 m) and 3 touchdowns. He was named Super Bowl MVP for the second time.

★ Key Players ★

There were other key players on the New England Patriots who helped win Super Bowl XXXVIII (38). Here are two of them.

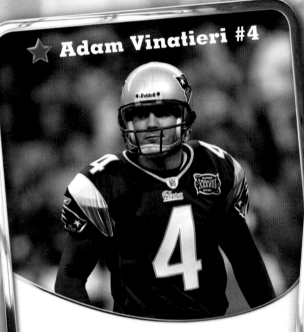

★ **Adam Vinatieri #4**

Position: Kicker

Born: 12/28/1972 in Yankton, South Dakota

Height: 6' 0" (1.83 m)

Weight: 202 pounds (92 kg)

Key Play: Kicked the game-winning field goal

★ **Deion Branch #83**

Position: Wide Receiver

Born: 7/18/1979 in Albany, Georgia

Height: 5' 9" (1.75 m)

Weight: 190 pounds (86 kg)

Key Plays: 10 catches for 143 yards (131 m), including the 17-yard (16-m) reception to set up the game-winning field goal

★ Glossary ★

backup (BAK-uhp)
a player who doesn't play at the start of a game

draft (DRAFT)
an event in which professional teams take turns choosing college athletes to play for them

field goal range
(FEELD GOHL RAYNJ)
the area of the field where a kicker is close enough to be able to make a field goal

interceptions (in-tur-SEP-shuhnz)
passes that are caught by players on the defensive team

kicker (KIK-ur)
the player who kicks the ball on kickoffs, field goals, and extra points

linebacker (LINE-bak-ur)
a defensive player who is on the second line, makes tackles, and defends passes

opponents (uh-POH-nuhnts)
athletes who people play against in a sporting event

Orange Bowl (OR-inj BOHL)
a famous college football game held each year in Miami, Florida

pocket (POK-it)
the area where a quarterback drops back to throw the ball

pressure (PRESH-ur)
a strain or burden

receivers (ri-SEE-vurz)
players who catch passes

sideline (SIDE-line)
an area where players stand during the game when they are not on the field

starting (START-ing)
playing at the beginning of a game; the best player at a position

turnovers (TURN-oh-vurz)
plays that result in the loss of the football to the other team

uprights (UHP-rites)
the two upward-pointing bars on the goalpost

Bibliography

Pierce, Charles P. *Moving the Chains: Tom Brady and the Pursuit of Everything.* New York: Farrar, Straus and Giroux (2006).

Sports Illustrated

www.boston.com/sports/football/patriots/superbowl2004/

www.patriots.com

Read More

Christopher, Matt. *The Super Bowl: 40 Years of Amazing Games.* New York: Little Brown and Company (2006).

Gigliotti, Jim. *Tom Brady.* Mankato, MN: Child's World (2007).

Wheeler, Jill C. *Tom Brady.* Edina, MN: Checkerboard Books (2006).

Learn More Online

To learn more about Tom Brady, the New England Patriots, and the Super Bowl, visit **www.bearportpublishing.com/SuperBowlSuperstars**

Index